Megaglorations

WESLEY FRANZ

Megaglorations

∞ MAIDA VALE PUBLISHING

First published in 2019
by Maida Vale Publishing Ltd
Suite 333, 19-21 Crawford Street
Marylebone, London W1H 1PJ
United Kingdom

Cover design and typeset by Edwin Smet
Printed in England by TJ International Ltd, Padstow, Cornwall

The right of Wesley Franz to be identified as author of
this work has been asserted in accordance with section 77
of the Copyright, Designs and Patents Act 1988

ISBN 978-1-912477-65-4

WWW.EYEWEARPUBLISHING.COM

dedicated to Malu Carmo – of course!!

Wesley Franz
has lived in São Paulo for many
years where he studied and graduated as an engineer.
He worked in industry for twenty-nine years. Recently,
he has been teaching and giving support in English for
his students, most of them physicians and PhD students
in fields relating to biology. His poetic influences include
W. Carlos Williams, Ted Hughes, Philip Larkin, Keats,
J. Cabral, C.D. Andrade and F. Pessoa, to name a few.
In 1969, as a teenager, he participated in a poetry contest
where he satirized the military of that time. These
shenanigans brought censorship and threats, and he
was told never to write verse again. Some years later
he started – and still is – disobeying. He loves regular
feijoada, and spends time chatting with friends
and sailing. Married, with a son and a daughter,
he writes whenever 'inspiration'
strikes – usually.

TABLE OF CONTENTS

INTRODUCTION

This collection brings some ideas and words that deserve simple explanations –

   a) Megagloration

Comes from Megalopolis plus Agglomeration – very big cities or urban spots relentlessly swelling around the world. From a rather simple point of view they feature positive, negative or neutral aspects. From an historical point of view, they seem somewhat terrifying and overwhelming.

   b) The Dragon

The last poem/story refers to an Animal/ Symbol very present, in different forms, in many countries. The classical image of a Christian Knight/Hero slaying the Dragon is absurd; the Dragon just can't be killed, as He lives (and always has) way beyond our mortal conceptions of Life and Death. Other images and sculptures of Dragons being 'slain' also become absurd. Hence, the Dragon represents mankind's fear of the Unknown. There is no reason whatsoever for this fear.

WORDS, WORDS, WORDS

Unspoken, silent
resilient, powerful.
Pregnant with ideas
words can be
heavy,
unsettling.

CAPITAL BREEZE

Breeze of happy ideas
flowing through the Mind
blowing away
useless thoughts
of material grandness
(Capital!! $$$!!)

Maybe too, too much
more and more and such
becomes less and less, but

There is
Imagination, which tends to be
Priceless

HE DID NOT GO TO WAR

Although they tried to draft him –
so far it's been 13 times that he
has undergone life-threatening episodes

Loaded guns six times faced
last one a rifle on the left ear
(Stop speeding you son of a bitch!!!
Sorry officer, I am late for...)

The almost-terminal illness, the gaze
of the nurse (shook her head with
such sincere pity – *this one is lost...*)
but again he survived and the
Grim Reaper did not really approach

A sea cruise on a regular motor boat
Gale strong from the southwest
twelve foot breakers from port and abaft
but his Dad was a hell of a Skipper
and saved both crew and the sturdy craft

Crazy car crashes add to the list
of that survivor's episodes.
Memories are resilient and strong
from life's umpteen roads

and one gets what destiny consigns.
Thus,
he now placidly writes these lines.

CHECKING OTHER POSSIBILITIES

And then on the not-so-far ahead –
when a lot of things shall be different
and deep internal bio-psychological questions
can be put in, say, numbers, we

Will be able to buy feelings
and attitudes in a supermarket
(happiness always on a discount,
rage mid-priced –
Sincerity? Only in non-transparent wrapping –
Solidarity – oh – somewhat expensive
and yet so hard to find...)

And we'll get home without any
confusion in our jocund minds

SKINNY GIRL

So frail she is, that skinny girl
certainly undernourished on her
very first year – family poor
devoid of means to provide
for life's crazy curvature

But her smile is wide.
Her glance is cute.
Now almost 20 she will
follow ahead – but other ones
still

won't have the same chances.
Won't have that smile wide,
and dead very young will not
join us in our now life-ride

FLUID MIRRORS

We tend to take 'em for granted.
Why mirrors?
Nicely explained by regular Physics.
See how they work:
The more you move away from them
the broader the image they forward
into our Imagination-Virtual

So, lesson number one:
The farther you move away
the more you can see

Ideas mirror

Ideas – universe, borderless they'll be if one
moves away from them...

Mankind mirrors

In this world
Fatherhood and mirrors are abominable
As they multiply the number of men
Just a plain fact.

Diving into

Dive into a Mirror-Lake-Pond
with calm water solemnly reflecting.
But you won't accept
that the farther you move
the more you can see.

Fluid mirror now destroyed.

But eventually water's surface
becomes still again –
There –
The Mirror reborn

probably abominable.

SOME REAL PEACE

Quietly observing nothing
pregnant with solemn sloth,
abstruse ideas slowly waning
like mushrooms in morning sun.

Such soft afternoon atmosphere.
Hardly any wind,
dressed in a hammock.
Caressing the words as if
they were new-born babies.

And then
(surely because of space-time awareness...)
Floating feelinglessly
towards mild semi-non-existence.

PERSPECTIVE OF CERTAIN THINGS

Moving through this desert
You spot a city in the Dis

                              tance.

The buildings, the skyscrapers
the structures, roads,
life, hermetic wonders
lie ahead and –
you know (or think you do)
all scientific facts about each molecule
(let alone the atoms) involved in the consolidation
of that
town-circumstance –
(not yet a Megagloration...)

You could be a little afraid.
You should be aware.
What have we Men made?

FULL MOON AND CONSEQUENCES

Full moon above
your
observation point.
A mirror in
the sky.

How many poets have produced
Nice Verse
under
The Moonlight...
The serious moonlight

Absolutely agree.
Just check
and you'll see.

DIFFERENT IDEAS

Differently from many
he (I) senses (sense)
some twenty years ago as
before yesterday

Maybe somewhat weird –
but, yes, very
very nice,
time.
Time and
again, profusely,
time.
How is that???

Have you ever felt it???
So, inside your body-age
will you face it calmly
without any funny rage??

WAYS OF WALKING THROUGH LIFE

It can be clearly seen that in the end
we are mere passengers of spaceship Earth
being just carried to Whatever

Sometimes in life you should stride.
Sometimes you can solemnly saunter.

May this platitude
be no hurdle
to your awareness
connected
with the wonders of this lark.

XMAS TREES HERE AND THEN

Looking at
maybe staring at
that regular Xmas tree,
he may feel
the power of fond old memories

Looking at
the news in the newspaper.
That ordinary newspaper.
He now reads
about clashes, guerrillas and deaths

And it's Xmas time.
And he feels sad.

Folding the newspaper under his arm he walks away.
Regardless if they believe or not.
Santa Claus will not show up if you've been
a naughty boy, or a warring, grown man.

Just naughty boys, assholes.
After all

SOME SCARS

Sometimes a survivor of
our sort of daily battles
conscious of those small

Wounds.

Carrying, but not showing,
scars of everyday life
that can slowly get smaller –
but never completely disappear

If he gets to old age
when the wrinkles of his skin
will be happily smiling
showing how good they are
in disguising that old scar

In the heart-soul inside, however,
you don't have those biological tissues
that help hiding external scars

You could caress them –
Scars in your heart-soul
and keep on thinking -
Pain – oh – oh – but no

Ain't self-pity
such a shitty
quagmire...??

Touch those scars inside you.
Find out that the tissues-ideas
grown and surrounding
the scars of your life
are of good quality
more flexible, able to make
yourself, heart-soul more
resilient.

Yeah, fuck, resilient, that's it.

BRIEF DESCRIPTION OF KA'S SMILE

He was gladly surprised
by your shining eyes.
Black eyes, deep as
black night bloated with
the mysteries of your soul.

And here that addictive combination
with this coltish smile of yours

Music irenically invaded
the way of his thoughts
making the whole picture-dimension
perfect, clear, blithesome
as the dawn of a new
day.

When everything starts –
again.

URBAN NEWSSTAND

Across the street it remains
displaying the dailies;
Plenty of Information.

One can buy a tumid magazine
that contains an essay covering
the soft aspects
of concrete poetry.

Or choose another one –
Pages of artistic photography
of buxom, callipygian girls.
Get a high on that one
and maybe some nice swirls.

Newsstand (issues notwithstanding) is
closing now.
More tomorrow about
same wars, insane strife
candid, simple part of
many an ordinary life

There it remains, not solemnly –
but stubbornly.

THE COLOUR GREEN

Is a combination of many reflections
of light rays – our
human eyes find it on
trees, fields, agriculture, meaning
food.
Forests, jungles, sometimes some seas and it
may allow

some mephitic ideas to slowly
disappear, if
everything works out fine.

We can then think blue
(it is close to green...)

THE OCEAN CRUISER

She observes the ocean ship
solemnly cruising the waters of that coast.
White, gorgeous and now dodgy
ready to disappear in the distance.

A floating city
exploring the space
of a non-city

      – The Ocean.

Majestic and forward moving
the Liner on the endless sea
could surely be a symbol of
what we REALLY want to be.

Resolute, excellent command
a precise bearing and a clear
purpose.

How romantic.
Just some words, naïve words.
Actually just some architecture floating
over non-cities.

But her dream is on.
Let's not disturb it.

FLY ON THE CHEESE

Placidly observing that
unloved animal as it
nourishes itself with
some protein, I guess.

So the fly can keep on
flying, living
being part of Nature –
pursuing
its role in Biology
(don't know which one here)

The marvel of Life on
that maybe pesky creature –
Cells, eyes, flying buzz
any other curious feature?

OK, now I
Kindly ask you, please –
Fuck off my cheese!!!

HUMMINGBIRD ON A LINE

Dusk.
Telephone line-wire stretched across
the garden.
Hummingbird lands and clings
to the line and starts

With its garrulous
Chip-chap   chip-chap
Chip-chip   chat-chat –
It sounds just like that.

Call for another hum'bird
now flying around him
also going   chip-chip
chip-chap   chip-chap

And I then realize,
checking the chip-chap,
this hummingbird must be
a rather smart chap –

Using the phone line-wire
precisely for the purpose
of transmitting messages –
Hum'birds and Humans: here alike

Chip-chat   chip-chat   nice talk, chat, chat

SOME DRIVING

Reinvent
    Readapt
        Reduce

And again reduce, down-shift
so that you won't spin on
that bend of your life.

And then carry on
with full throttle.

Rekindle
    Rethink
        Reconstruct

That old relationship
so that you won't cry on
Someone's soft shoulder –
found a comfortable boulder?

You will be able to choose.

RAIN AND OBSERVATIONS

It has been raining now
for 37 hours, 37 mins and 46 seconds
now; yes, 51 seconds
over everyone.

Dogs, cars, houses and fields.
It rains on, on the people
wielding umbrellas and

on the Policemen with those
potent potentially life-extinguishing-machines
handy out of their macs.

Hope one day they won't be needed anymore.
No Cops, no Soldiers, no Judges, no Prisons.
No bandits, no swindlers, no violent bores;
just a few basic, well-accepted silent mores

But then still
need the rain
yes we will.

COLOURS AROUND US

The ocean was blue
the Sky another blue.
The boat with its normal
light grey and yellow

white sails
white as my thoughts.
Peaceful,
placidly white

The breeze is transparent
which doesn't mean it is
devoid of colour

it's just we can't see it.
It's funny to observe that
it's difficult to check
transparent things which otherwise you
feel.
And it is not only the breeze...
Wow!! many other things...

Maybe some crazy stuff
can help seeing enough...

LESSONS FROM THE PARK

There is the park and pertaining pond-lake
surrounded by
park – with its regular features –

pond-lake, built by us
as with so other many things...

Our unsurprising Bum-Beggar sitting on
his unsurprising bench-home, when
two Men from the religious area
(priests, preachers, whatever)
try to cajole him to regular life as I
walk by.

On the pond-lake floats a black swan
quietly drifting above
the filthy water, so
spontaneous in his stolid Majesty.
I walk by.

Elderly lady reading a book, oblivious
of Baby screaming in the pram beside her –
(Must be a very good book...)
I walk by

Regular pigeons fly above.

Regular beggar over there.
(Priests were not successful...)
Reading lady moved along.

And the black swan solemnly
keeps on drifting by
floating effortlessly on
and above
the soiled water.
Now – that's one attitude there...

Let's learn.
I walk by.

VAMPIRES AND BIOLOGY

Night, and the Vampire goes
flying, walking or crawling
ordinary chore – chasing dinner –
sinister –
moving through darkness...

Poverty in our soul
prevents us from finding
power for the future.
Propose a solution: There

goes the Vampire our
half-Man half-Idea conception
executing redemption of our sins
craving for Immortality through
digestion of younger blood.

Our future we don't know.
Vampires float by –
what an oddly nice show.

TALKING TO ONESELF

That adamant capacity of talking to him/herself
using written words, rhymes, rhythm, expressions
express his/her sometimes mild craziness and how it
tends to be slightly offbeat, just as one would
normally expect of people who talk a little too
much to themselves using their sound-making
features like tongue, lips, mouth and voice.

Some admit these traits.
Others just not really so.

These last ones could be analyzed.
Maybe clinically, who'll know?

HOUSES, HOMES

Were created in that old
neighbourhood where the
pebbbbbbbbledashed semis exist

and still, old, nice
memories duly persist

Unfathomable through time
because of the huge
number of emotions (humane? human?)
that once pervaded
(still pervading!!! still pervading!!!)
these intimate architectural structures.

Someday they
will be razed down, systematically, to
allow space for
tall buildings penetrating
vertical space (Megagloration!!)
instead of old
horizontal, earthly
house-homes.

Yes, we must be very apt
to then blithely adapt.

HEADLINES – 'NEWBORN POEM IS...'

A recent poem was abandoned
by the creator on an empty
grass field

Recklessly as a crazy mother
leaves behind her newborn in
the Hands of Destiny.

Wind blows and renders the poem
airborne –
candid leaf of paper floating
innocently on the atmosphere
landing in the hands of someone's destiny
who reads, likes and under-signs it.

There, new fatherhood –

STRANGE ANIMALS

At night the bat flying, squeaking to
find the right direction using
sound waves – sonar safely
navigating through darkness.

Darkness in Man's soul
doesn't allow as a whole
to decide our destiny.
Devise a solution: over

soars the Vampire –
exercising on redemption of our sins
craving for immortality at
the expense of FOREIGN BLOOD...

Bats are great survivors
without quest for immortality –
flying around, mostly not caring
about that other creature – Man.

There they are – three strange creatures –
solicitous at times, perhaps,
all three of them...

NEW MACHINES

That horrifying possibility
when machines will 'think'
(we won't have to think anymore...)
The machines (once called computers)
eventually will solve our normal
daily problems including our
needs for existence like, say,
food, water, sex and laughter
(can't live without laughter...)

But

it may be that – horrifying possibility –
we'll have our greatest trait pilfered:
this thing nicely called creativity.

HAPPY DISCOVERY

Delving into his
pockets
he finds a nice banknote
good to pay some old debts.

Delving into his pockets he
finds
some scribbled stuff that he
immediately translates
according to his now-feelings, and
it was
about
that nice surprise of finding

A poem in one's pockets.

A poem in everyone's mind...
Sincere, candid, unaligned...

ANOTHER PHONE CALL

He calls and gets the answering machine –
Please leave your message after the beep
'Ka, are you there? See, I just want
to talk to someone.
My landlord said I must leave tomorrow
as my rent is long overdue
Where would I go, I ask you,
being penniless ain't no crime –

And, oh, my faithful motorbike
was mangled by a lorry – beyond
repair – What should I do?
I just want to talk to someone
instead of feeling crazily blue.

Remember me dog?
Old' ...
                    Beep beep beep beep ...

'Hello? Oh, the machine, yeah,
it's me again – well, the beloved
dog, old companion, old friend
died yesterday – I'm so alone –
please understand –
I really had to phone.

Ask about my sis, she
is in hospital, they say,
with baleful Destiny
ready to take her away.

So, as you see, it
seems I've got a number
of problems to cope with
and, yeah, I won
the lottery yesterday
More than half a million
And' ...

Beep beep beep beep ...

'All right, all right, it's me
again, see,
I just wanted
to talk to someone...'

POLLUTED STREAM

Let's analyze all
the stuff found in a filthy stream
abandoned, maybe floating
(this you can see)
maybe dumped and sunk
(this you must imagine)

           Check there what used to be
a mattress, a chair, a radio,
plastic bags loaded with trash –
a headless doll, a pair of shoes
(mysteriously bound together)
a broken brown broom,
a book, so unequivocally forgotten...

How sad.
This once water-body
now just a despicable bog-like thing
its almost no-flow drifting
like a sad tear tracking down
the face of
a quasi-dead zombie.

Yes, a zombie.
And like a zombie
it can be revived.

EXPOSED NERVE

He is a walking man on the surface of Earth.
Non-oblivious man, sensitive –
Sometimes way toooooo much so…

Lambasted by
the blunders of other men.

Wafting along
these almost-adventures of our lives.
He's got this condition, you see,
lots of that sometimes painful
over-sensitivity

UNHAPPY SITUATION

A waitress She is
working in a nice joint
smiling to clients
cleaning tables, serving around –
that is her job, honestly found.

Boarding the underground
wearing that candid smile She
arrives at premises
people call 'Home'.

Gets beaten and cursed by
a drink-too-many husband.

She'll take pain her way
silent tears roll down –
Kids are sleepin' – it's OK.

Let us be aware, aware, aware
it just shouldn't happen
shouldn't happen, no, anywhere.
Can we care, yes, care, care...

ADDICTIONS, ADDICTIONS

She is addicted to
her more-than-daily
drink   that
makes her feel happy but
she is striving to give up.

He is on the horse Addiction
watching the races
hoping one evening it
won't happen anymore
(like the pack-a-day smoke)

Now that other fellow
is addicted to verse-writing.
Terminally hopeless he
doesn't care about it.

CAT IN THE NIGHT

Ta-ta-ta the prowler's prowess is admired
no nice sleep and stuff –
Hey baby, come on, let's be biological
and make some kittens old fashion' way.

Just species survival –
Meeou. Meeou
– all of me.
Now.

WITHOUT A NUMBER OF THINGS

No money.
No shoes.
No credit.
No clues –

Damn the money
call old friends –

Between him and Real Life
a separation
with the width of big oceans.
But then he shall never be
lackadaisically bereft of emotions

OBSERVATION ON OBSERVATIONS

Most people observe
only partially
or, perhaps,
pretend just doing so
to give the impression
of how much they know.

One should check that this can be
partially fake (at least). Where is
that complete specialist, abundant
with sapience galore?
But what has he really got
in his intimate hard core?

WE MISS THE BIG CITY

When away in a smaller cluster
we miss the air pollution to which
we became pleasantly addicted.
And the blithe noise of cars, planes,
choppers, screams, cats and dogs, madmen.

Unnecessary to greet all people in the Megagloration,
so the false, foolish grins
can be avoided.
You don't know everybody, so remain
comfortably dressed in sincere oblivion.

Are big cities Darwinian? Connected with evolution
of species, our species and other ones?
A father is there murdered and his young children
will have to adapt.
Rats in big city sewers are
smarter than their cousins from the wild.

Megagloration stray dog checks one of his kin
run down and crushed when carelessly crossing
a busy avenue – doggie learns about moving vehicles...

Maybe big cities are here for
a biological reason...

OF JOURNEYS AND WRITINGS

Both start with an Idea-Design-Project.

With that very first old step.
With that very first line
igniting same mild fears
and maybe ideas to shine.

We ought to continue
maybe fast, maybe slow.
But definitely, certainly
we really must go.

NOISE AND A FRIEND…

He is devoid of ideas in his mind.
Just noise.
Noise of the people.
Noise of the telephone.
Noises of voices –

voices.

Voices of people from today
or of folks who've gone away.
Voices, some for the long run –
remember voices, voices
can be nice, can be fun
(old memories just begun…)

PLEASANTLY ARRIVING SOMEWHERE

Why do we need emotions?
Can you give a reason?
Try a psychological, biological
sociological or
whateverological explanation.

He,
the Scribbler,
having checked 'this Moon, this Brandy'
gets touched and moved.

Hence the yearning for emotions.

THE HEART UNDER

That resilient Heart
now almost devoid of mendacity
through a quasi-lifetime
of experiences, good and bad
but all instructive.

That resilient Heart
sometimes forlorn
most times hopeful.
Yeah, hopeful...

Perhaps mawkishly so –
OK, all right:
Just a little mawkish.
Just a little.

SELECTIVE SHAMES

Check around and see
if 10,000 years of civilization
mean somethin' more than it should. Should what?

Painfully yet positively aware
of our beastly origins,
of our natural past.
And 'natural' becomes a drossy word.

Those wily, gangster-like
apes, the ancestors of our ancestors.
Natural selection at work, the fittest made it.
First only the strongest
and then probably the smartest.

500,000 machetes in the heart of the jungle,
half a million (more, more...) humans hacked to death.
Just another butchery in history.
Maybe natural selection?
Stubbornly untamed, pervasively at large.

Ten thousand years of civilization,
philosophy, science, airplanes
splitting the atom, literature, super-strings

but

the relentless bio-selfish ape
remains

inside of everyone.
Certainly more present and
unaware of
that shitty n... selection.

That's the task, the quest
to continuously transform –
can we do our very best
and crush the bio-norm?

Less human,
but more, way more
humane.

AMAZING PLANS

The plan is to grab, grab, grab
a glass of wine and
a nice verse from William Carlos Williams
then take off for the realms of 47.33% omniscience.

Try to rein in that smothering sense of
the heart in the throat
(Have you felt it sometimes?
Then express!! Express!!!)

Then tell the World to go fuck, fuck, fuck
But he
just can't, can't, can't...

THE FIVE POUND STORY REVISITED

He's got only two fivers in his pocket
but an old feeling – pain in his mind
so
he is just too busy to think about anything
else.

Let alone money.

RECENT HISTORY

How has our mind evolved in the last
nine thousand nine hundred and
ninety-nine years?

Big money people seldom think of this.
It is understandable most don't care...
It may be too complex (well...)
Shit happens almost everywhere.

WAGGISH AWARENESS

The sun shines.
Nuclear fusion.
So simple.

Brings an illusion.
Nice day?
The atmosphere's ways are chaotic.
Be careful not to let simple task-beliefs
turn out like something quixotic...

GROWING UP AND GROWING

There once was a boy
who liked to check birds
birdies singing, flying around.

And that boy inexorably grew up
so the birds had to be traded
for the reality of the world.
Soft dreams slowly disappeared.

They had to give place to
awareness of Kalashnikovs galore
dangerous as meretricious politicians

But then after years and years
birds are still around.
They do, singing or not,
bring out a lovely sound
from inside the deep soul
with peace again found.

WEAPONS, WEAPONS AND MORE

There was a man with a club,
a silent form of POWER and persuasion.

There was a man with a sword
ready to cut and to bring
execution, evolution.

There is a man with a gun
power from powder.
Nice shot, uncanny death.

There is a man with a missile
coldly fired into the night.
Target, target, doesn't matter the
many many people killed.

There is a man with a pen and paper
and ideas –
Will they ever be more powerful than weapons??
These times... these times.

SCHADENFREUDE AND CONSEQUENCES

In Roman times we had it there galore
damn the Gladiator, damn the Retiarius.
One of them has to get fucked up,
cut into pieces, the crowd wants more.

Round here, this now capitalistic situation when
one gets broke and the so-called friends
say
Oh, how bad...
Purest form of insincerity.

Or maybe not

Perhaps this is bloody innate to us.
Perhaps it is just this.

They love to watch the soap opera, film
when the good guys get screwed up
and in the end
everything is OK.

Obviously we have all experienced
that Schadenfreude – if for just
a second or so.
Admit it –

Their city was victimized
with dreadful crazy planes inserting
themselves into the Towers, but
it was THEIR city

Yeah, I am so smart
oh so bloody smart
not to live there...

And then there was a flood.
Big one this time.
THOUSANDS of dead people.
'Twas THEIR country
not my neighbourhood.

Yeah, I am so smart
oh so bloody smart
not to live there...

You've got it in your inside –

Schadenfreude, love it, hate it, digest it.

THE NEW GUEST

He found a mouse
in his 'dwelling-place'
(just to avoid the obvious, vapid rhyme)

In there (now his house) there was a
new inhabitant, a citizen
of that big city which features
a big lot of those creatures.

He did not care about it
but others really did
and they acted to get rid
of the new Mickey aboard.

And so Mr Mickey was duly
poisoned and dying he
was found and cared about.

Laid on a white paper to become
the last shroud, the mouse's last breaths.
He filled his glass and spared a last sip
served to the dying animal so to go
into the afterworld drunk and happy.
The small white teeth delivered a grin.

Off to the streets, he has to
provide Mr Mickey with a proper burial.
Clad in the white paper-shroud
not even a pound weight.
Now dead, but probably happy
in its own concept of this
which we dare not discuss.
He was solemnly dropped
into a regular gutter not
like the so many once-citizens
who lose their lives in such
crazy ways and do not
have a proper shroud to
caress their death.

Mr Mouse I do respect.
He was just like me,
a Megagloration citizen,
a survivor by profession.
Fending off threats, problems and
many kinds of oppression...

INSTRUCTIONS FOR A LONELY DEATH

When death is the very last door
you can see ahead of you
and your so-friends label you a bore
with all else rendered insignificant.

Tell 'em you are sick.
(They don't care...)
Tell 'em you need a talk
(They're just not there...)

Find yourself a new illness
an infection caused by your
own infected mind and you
go to hospital and confirm
that you're very ill
and you don't give a fuck.

They'll try to heal you.
But you don't want to live
and eventually make it, peacefully,
to the other side not

disturbing, oh, no one,
Except
me here, last one.

OTHER LESSONS FROM OTHER PARK

It didn't snow yesterday.
Early morning, the sun
insists on driving positive beams
into our minds, so I walk by

There is a man jogging!!!
Big smile on his face and
after every thirty seconds he yells
Hello, hello to you hello, hello
somewhat unhinged –
definitely happy.

Mr Elderly there playing chess
with himself as his himself partner-adversary
makes a move, changes sides
talks to his other self with a
funny grin on the side of his mouth –
'Nah!! You won't get me there...'
But don't we all sometimes play
games with ourselves?

Now check that very small dog
smelling the private parts of
another very BIG dog...
Quite natural, you suppose.
Quite courageous, I say.

Now, what about that young Lady
dressed in her leotard that
enhances her features
talking (no, yelling) on
her mobile with
probably now an ex-lover.
Or maybe someone else –
Who knows? (Let imagination run free...)

There is a quiet Lady sitting on a bench
check her gaze watching the planets above...
(It is daylight!!! daylight!!)
But placidly observing her eyeball
you get the image of Uranus...

There is a man taking a picture, a photograph
of this nice, salutary morning in the park.
Maybe that portrait will become
more diaphanous than these lines.

KISSES & LOVING COUPLES

We watch 'em on the telly.
We check them in the Movies.
We usually find them *Oh – so Romantic*
and tend to smile when we see them –
OH!! Shall love prevail!!

We actually don't know them
but they are human beings...

A loving couple with kisses
unconsciously takes our minds
away to the suggestion that
after the kisses (when? when?)
There may be...

And here it is –
most of us most unconsciously like
to check the continuation of this our species.
It is biological, natural
within us...

So next time you see some real good kissing
(D. Kerr & B. Lancaster remain unbeaten...)
think of it as a good thing as
some genes and some minds will be One.

TOOTHPASTE AND CONTROVERSY

He gets ready to sleep.
Tooth brushing, no toothpaste,
so as not to spoil the last flicker
of that tasty wine.

He gets ready to dream
dreaming of talking to Mr Jung
about
his previous dream.

Trying to construe the
interpretation of the Grand Master
he'll have a

dream within a dream –
a rather riveting scene.

Hey, that's cool –
Try it, maybe you can...

AFTERNOON'S FUNCTION

If one has the whimsical feeling of
this (any, any...)
Afternoooooon, time of the day

It is peculiar.
Feel it, feel it,
not intensively,
but placidly...

Sun is out!!!
Peace...
In this case
In this case...

Just a feeling of a peaceful afternoon...

Peaceful???? These days?????????

RECURRING CHALLENGE

There was a Nice Idea
drifting on
the oceans of her mind.

The tides of life
just took it away, as it often happens.

Go sailing after it!!
But, then, maybe,
not now...

We'll wait for the good breeze
so that we won't need to
give the mind a tight squeeze
and quietly allow the nice wind
to take us away with gallant ease

DEMOCRACY, DEMOCRACY

Democracy

Power to the people
Power to the people

Elections.

You decide that
your candidate will do
THE thinking for you

Democracy
Ok???
You'll have to think about how
Your candidate shall do
future thinking for you.

HOW TO SOLVE PROBLEMS INSIDE

It is quite easy –
find the carrion in
your mind and
get
one
diligent BUZZARD-Idea

to eat it up –

He will be happy to help you.

THE FROG AND THE LITTLE VERSE

A short poem was in his mind –
maybe five or six lines,
but like a frog on the edge of a pond,
ready to jump into it,
that little poem jumped into oblivion.

Blame the conversation.
The lack of pen and paper
the need to concentrate on ordinary shit...
traffic, whatever,
it just jumped out of perspective.

Have to wait till it
resurfaces, but then maybe a little
different...
Who could then know?
Will it oracularly grow?

LONG, LONG TIME NO SEE

It's been 37 years
since he last saw his ol' friends
on one of life's fortuitous bends.
Now we talk again and relate
the hindrances of our fate.

And also about the good things –
yeah, there have been some good things

Hope is this pervasive feeling
We're both a bit weird,
but not that crazy...

Like the phoenix,
out of the so-called ashes of life
Friends will soar again.
High.

NEW SUMMER AND SUMMERS

It is
summer again, summer again, summer again!
We can get our Bermuda shorts and...
Go commando, go commando, go commando,
and every new summer is
hotter than the last one, hotter than the last one.

We know (or we think we know)
why this is so, why is this so
but
we don't care, we don't care.

Well, we should be
bloody aware, bloody aware.

Nature will undoubtedly
charge a
heavy fare, heavy fare.

RESCUE OPERATION

So you can observe
many people in places of
power and possibility
(Presidents, P. Ministers and more)

Possibility to change things
for the best
for evolution, improvement
of
this obtuse bio-happening
called the human race

However...
most of them are
unpardonably trapped in the Bog of Insensitivity
– Shall we build lifelines with candid words to show
that we can get them out of that deplorable slough?

THE SIZE OF THE DRAGON

I. Intro, sort of

Actually, the Dragon has many sizes
He is here, there
and almost
everywhere...
You pretend you don't know him
but then yes, you do
He's also inside of you

Part of mankind, today,
has forgotten the Dragon. But,
now and then,
someone has to remind us
remind us of some, say, Universalities...

2. *The story of the Dragon*

Although for the Dragon history might be
irrelevant, for us (who insist on being mortals)
it can be rather significant, so,
be aware that the Dragon has been around
long before we, mankind, were to be found
on this planet. Then, when we've figured
ourselves oh so superior in the face of the
other creatures that infested this Earth
(whales and cockroaches included)

Well, the Dragon was already here.
We knew then and sort of did revere
with that fulgent, inherent bit of fear.

Merlin the Magician
(knowing the Dragon and the
Power he
yielded, maybe displayed) was
aware of the Dragon's kind pervasiveness.
Merlin was a friend of the Dragon.
Wise men still tend to be
(tend to be, tend to be...)

3. *The Dragon among us*

Always among and around us
but never conspicuous
the Dragon inhabits the depths of
the atom or fermions or quarks.
Name all the subatomic particles
and the Dragon smiles...

The Dragon has no social issues.
He placidly mingles with creatures
of different biology and skin colours –
different ideas – He is them all!!
Take it easy, you can be
His nice, regular, cool pal

Take all literature, all wars
The bio-psychological aspects of Human Relations

And the Dragon smiles...

      We (mankind) have found the
new genome for, whatever,
and the
Dragon softly smiles

(Remember Merlin: the Dragon is our friend)

Many have tried to
understand the Dragon.
They pictured it, depicted in many
forms, wings, tails and the obvious
flaming mouth
(a symbol? a symbol?)

But
then they tried to count the number of
Dragons –
and again, no problem as
The Dragon is Much and Many.

Which takes us to
Oh, the

4. *The Mathematics of the Dragon*

Probably in face of all probabilities
this area seems to be
very possibly
post-fractal

Yeah, all Mathematics could be
included in the Dragon.

The Dragon is all Mathematics
that we know
so far

(Far is here a very, very small thing)

5. Check the Dragon in the Smile of Children

The Dragon knows the meaning of Children
(translates as Hope – it is so, so inherent...)
But, again, He smiles and cares.

6. Other aspects of the Dragon

And then Alpha is not a constant
(the fine structure one) anymore
Hey, here the Dragon says *Helloooo!!!*
What do we think we know???
Superstrings?
For the Dragon, an easy show

Agriculture, yes agriculture –
When it then came by
people got a bit Dragon-shy.
Less hunger meant less need
for magic, and hence the awareness
of the Dragon did then recede...

But of course He didn't care

as He had (still has)
Lots of power to spare.

And, yeah,
twice lambent the Dragon is –
on his candid light
for your own insight.

7. Continuation

Years going by, centuries passing are
of relative importance to the Dragon
(He sort of cares about us as any friend would!!)

Remember Merlin
Remember the
Magic.

This magic of the unknown.

Find the Dragon!!!

Find it here and everywhere 'cos
The Dragon is Much and Many.
Find the Dragon inside and outside –
The magic of the unknown.
The mystery.

The Fear –

So to open, non-diffident eyes
splendid Dragon will appear
regardless of, oh, form or size...

ACKNOWLEDGEMENTS

Thanks to Alex Wylie, Todd Swift and
Edwin Smet.